Qwerty

Acknowledgements

All the poems in this collection have previously been published. Several have won prizes in open competition, including 'The Mauve Tam-o'-Shanter' which won the *Times Literary Supplement* award in 2007.

Acumen, Ambit, Anglo-Welsh Review, Areté, Border Country, Borderlines, Bradford Poetry Quarterly, Brando's Hat, Country Quest, Critical Survey, Dreamcatcher, Envoi, Iota, Konfluence, Leviathan Quarterly, London Magazine, New Welsh Review, Orbis, Poetry Digest, Poetry London, Poetry Nottingham, Poetry Review, Poetry Scotland, Poetry Wales, Roundyhouse, Scintilla, Smiths Knoll, Thames Poetry, The Coffee House, The Dark Horse, The Frogmore Papers, The Interpreter's House, The New Writer, The North, The Rialto, The Shop, The Times Literary Supplement, Thumbscrew, Ware Competition Anthology, Wilkins Memorial Competition Anthology.

'Anglo-Welsh' was commissioned by the Hay-on-Wye Festival of Literature.

The author is grateful for grant aid from The Arts Council of Wales.

I am indebted to Amy Wack
for her ongoing support and editorial skill.

PAUL GROVES

Qwerty

seren

Seren is the book imprint of
Poetry Wales Press Ltd.
57 Nolton Street, Bridgend, Wales, CF31 3AE
www.seren-books.com

The right of Paul Groves to be identified as
the author of this work has been asserted in accordance
with the Copyright, Designs and Patents Act, 1988.

ISBN 978-1-85411-459-4

A CIP record for this title is available from the British Library.

The publisher acknowledges the financial assistance of the Welsh Books Council.

Cover Art:
Teresa Cholmondeley, The Cholmondeleys Dance Company
www.thecholmondeleys.org
Photo: Chris Nash. www.chrisnash.net
Body Language: Theresa Cholmondeley at the Chisenhale Studios, London, 1990,
published in *From A Glance At The Toes* by Chris Nash (Creative Monochrome).
Poet Portrait: Lorraine Bewsey. www.lorrainesartstudio.co.uk

Printed in Bembo by Bell and Bain, Glasgow

Contents

My Family and Mr Okudo

None of us had a suit. He had several.
We smelt, and he smelt, but his smell
came from Milan, and he bought it
from a shop we could never enter. He said,
"Welcome to my world. My game show
is your stairway to the stars. I offer
a house worth many yen, two cars,
a foreign holiday. I require your grandmother,
that is all." We said yes; she beamed –
a seventy-nine-year-old who presides over
our insanitary shack beneath an approach path
to Haneda Airport. Within a week
a sports coach was training her to keep a ball
airborne for fifty bounces without it falling.
On the day of the programme we were tense
with expectancy. She had tried, tried, tried
– and in rehearsal had succeeded. We sensed
that fate was netting us, like eels
in a foul canal, and transferring us
to clearer water. Mr Okudo looked confident,
but of what: her success or her failure?
I liked how the cameras glided across the smooth
studio floor, like soap across the base of the first
shower I had used in ages. My hair
was no longer matted; my scalp no longer itched.
My children ate their first American ice cream
in the spotless canteen. Our poverty
was sliding towards the edge of the abyss, thanks
to kind Mr Okudo and his production team.
The audience were electric, urging
the old lady to perform without error.
We waited in the wings. She tripped
into the spotlight. An electronic drum roll;
a call for silence. Above us many suns
were turned off; only one burned into the moment,
illuminating the red sphere she lifted
tremulously. It rose into the air, descending
only to rise again, and again, and again.
Mr Okudo's smile had not changed in the slightest.

Kington Encounter

Having paid a mystic a month before
to assess my personality
using tarot cards, and a bowl of water
by which to scry futurity,
I was taken aback at The Burton Hotel
when a Scotsman guarding his pint
was able, without any clue, to tell
me about myself to the point
of uncanniness. Such eldritch power
raised the hairs on my nape, and sent
a shudder from head to toe. Asked where
he obtained this skill, he bent
forward and tapped the side of his nose
in a close, conspiratorial pose.

Lord Palmerston's Demise

(18th October 1865: Brocket Hall, Hertfordshire)

I am having a supernatural experience, hovering
above the billiard table my body has expired on.
Here is the parlour maid squeezing from under
my hot corpse, semen on her thigh. It is the game of life
we have been playing on this baize: appropriation
of the weak by the strong, of a woman by a man,
of the heathen by the civilised British of whom I am
foremost representative (Her Majesty would forgive
my flight of egotistic fancy). When my heart stopped
moments ago the paroxysm of consummation
became unearthly. I have passed on in trouserless
morning dress, the expensive glint of pocket-
watch chain underscoring class ascendancy.
Her pubic tuft has a beguiling simplicity redolent of
Dark Continent girls who expose more than their teeth
and the whites of their eyes. I am suddenly ethereal:
cirrus cloud betokening a change for the worse...
cannon smoke downwind from the Spithead Review...
a swirl of Seidlitz powder in a glass....
How light I seem, freed from the biliousness of existence,
her breasts' magnetism, fear cupped in her irises.
The wainscoted wall supports a cue-rack,
the Indian table a tantalus containing port and Madeira;
inches away loom my library's topmost shelves.
What happens next I neither know nor care, only that
history books maintain discretion down the centuries.
Henry John Temple. Man of integrity. Died in office.

The New Axminster

The carpet fitter, on his hands and knees
at a skirting board, reminds her how
her husband was at midnight. The disease
of longing makes her crave fulfilment *now.*
She clears her throat, and asks, "Coffee or tea?"
He kneels upright, pencil behind an ear,
and stipulates the former, privately
wishing for the iced fizz of a beer.
Nightdress, housecoat, slippers: it would take
seconds to undress, to feel his power
pumping into her. "A piece of cake?"
He shakes his head. She realigns a flower
on the mantelpiece, and eyes his back.
Like Vulcan he administers a tack.

Grans 'R' Us Sounded A Good Idea

though Soay was rather remote, and Loch Scavaig
could get choppy. "You pronounce it 'Soy'"
said my partner. "There's no crime, the scenery
is exemplary, pollution is zero, the pace of life
relaxes and refreshes." We took her across on the boat
from Elgol. She huddled in the cabin, five large cases
at her feet like supplicants: over seven decades zipped
and belted in leather as grey as the waves.
After three miles in Hell's Cradle the vessel entered
the calmer waters of Camas nan Gall. Mrs Bechstein
stood on the jetty, ready to receive our first cheque.
A dozen senior citizens were accommodated here.
Denied the banality of bingo and television,
they awaited death like brave philosophers.
Clouds jostled for position to witness our disembarkation.
We stayed an hour. "You'll settle in quickly,"
we chimed. Our host watched us darkly
from the far side of the lounge. The monthly coaster
from Arisaig would bring supplies. Gulls would keen
for those who had gone before. Winds would preclude
outdoor use of the Zimmer. Arthritic fingers would wrestle
with knitting, slack lips accept a wee dram at bedtime.
The lawn had been consecrated for burials. Mrs Bechstein
had been authorised to officiate at each rapid interment.
As we chugged towards the mainland we remembered
those happy suburban years nothing could touch.

Strewth

On the plane to Sydney
her face was puffed and red.
I sat beside her for a while.
"Give me some space," she said.

On Bondi and on Manley
her eyes were hard as lead.
I held her hand along the sand.
"Give me some space," she said.

Our honeymoon was pretty strange.
We did not share a bed.
When I crept in beside her
"Give me some space" she said.

Eventually we reached Ayers Rock,
a massive loaf of bread
baked by the sun before Man walked.
"Give me some space," she said.

Distraught, I paid a guide to take
her out where no roads led –
the back of Bourke – and leave her there.
"Give her some space," I said.

The Roman Punishment for Parricide

Elements are in place for an execution. There are
no mitigating circumstances (the defendant's
'insanity' plea is disallowed). An arbiter,
striding the quay with a scroll headed SPQR,
will oversee proceedings dispassionately.
Below, slavering waves demand just deserts;
the Tyrrhenian Sea seems hungry for the prisoner
to appear. Three cages await, a clarion call
from one; from the next, gibbering; from the third
the rasp of a child's rattle – only deadlier.
Nearby is folded a sack made of material grown
on the malarial Agro Pontino. A cry resounds
as the bound man is brought forth. A caïque bobs
offshore; the party will be rowed out to it.
Legionary, magistrate, both oarsmen, murderer,
cock, monkey, and snake embark. The soldier
restrains the captive, whose appeals are unavailing.
The primate chatters; the reptile lies coiled; the fowl
flutters in its confinement but does not crow.
How beautiful the morning is! The group transfer
to the larger boat. Soon it will float so distantly
that the shore will become a smudge of charcoal.
The simian Symbol of Trickery, the anguine
Symbol of Evil, the pennate Symbol of Insolence,
and the Accused will be lowered in their bag
until brine claims their argument with themselves.
By then Sol will have reached his zenith.

Brain Drain

(85% of grey matter is water)

Two glasses of water are playing chess.
Two raindrops are making love:
watch them coalesce
where push comes to shove.

Your eyes water over the diced shallots
– which are mostly water. Words
flow down the page. Wet's
the ultimate adjective. Birds

take their aqueous bodies overhead.
The slug underfoot is as fluid as pus.
Oceans are haunted by the drowned dead.
We are water: water is us.

Adam's ale is on tap in the first garden.
The world is a soft drink, or else steam.
Clouds are doubt caused by the sun's
certainty. Time is a stream

issuing forever from the holy well
in the eternal hillside. Jesus is sleeping
in a flotation tank, unable to sink, while
Mary is weeping.

Falling off the Chrysler Building

Bloomington, Illinois is his town.
His father has been a construction worker too.
"Think tall, son, that's the shape of the future"
so Harry makes it to New York.
Walter P. Chrysler, having established his corporation,
finalises plans for free enterprise and egotism
to take towering form on Lexington and 42nd:
"It'll be the highest goddamn structure in the world!"
Harry rolls up his sleeves, spits on his hands.
The glint in his eye shows eagerness and commitment.
"You're hired!" the foreman barks as if aitches were f's.
"Yessir," shouts the new employee. Today his feet
will hardly touch the ground. William Van Alen, the architect,
has blueprints approved; foundations are laid; the dream
materialises. Labourers work feverishly, the race being on
to belittle H. Craig Severance, Van Alen's rival.
Art-Deco gargoyles resembling hubcaps;
Edward Trumball brilliantly painting the foyer;
and Harry in mid-air, halfway down
the seventy-seven storeys,
his colleagues' features chiselled into shock.
The skyscraper is topped out in 1930:
red ribbon, pink champagne, white teeth.
Harry's are in his buried remains in Bloomington
as autumn's first winds sweep across from Lake Michigan
and a grieving father, face and hair grey,
turns his greatcoat collar up.

Campanologists

It is as if they are milking the idea
of angels, trying to draw down heaven
through the tower with the strain
they are creating, cancelling fear

of the grave's silence by railing against
a mute God via the bells' din,
the raucous tintinnabulation
that airs their complaints

and grievances for over an hour
while they stand in a circle, facing
each other, wordlessly embracing
thick ropes which transmit power

to unseen clappers as twilight falls
around the church like a soft mist
completely at odds with each red fist
and the manic rhythm, the crazed pulse

of complaint and entreaty, ringing the changes
yet still getting nowhere other than bed
 – that linen tomb – when all is said
and done: the patterns, the exchanges.

Chess

You love her, but she lets you down. She has been
with Hungarians, Poles, American diplomats, students
from Havana, ranchers on the flanks of the Great Divide....
Her tastes are catholic and extend across the piano keys
of society: base hobos up to tinkling lounge lizards.
Fascists have demanded her presence and sat
savouring small drinks, fingering her fastidiously.
Overbred rarities in Hapsburg castles have kept her company
by the light of a sickly moon. Swashbucklers have sallied
forth at dawn on milky steeds, her derring-do in their breasts.
She is infuriatingly pliable, as accessible to my rival
as to me. You cannot bank on her. When she seems
to be in your lap she swaps allegiances. She eggs on
and breaks hearts. Who her parents were need not
detain us: they were probably travellers, gypsies,
charlatans with ways to make men weep, dance,
and lose their money. Spell weavers. Deceivers.
Chess has claimed me once too often on more
than one occasion. Why do I want to see her again?
Intimates say she is destructive of peace of mind,
anybody's, untrustworthy, possibly a carrier
of rare strains of madness and decay. That I risk
because I know, despite everything, she has beauty,
like those camel caravans, at dawn, at rest.

Bungalow Boy

I never went up the wooden hill
to Bedfordshire. My childhood lacked
stairs, the age-old Heaven-Hell
dichotomy of ascent and descent. Locked

into a horizontal plane, I crept
along the corridor to the end bedroom,
barefoot, shift-clad, Scrooge-capped,
once night had begun to begrime

the sky with its charcoal stick.
"Down Sheet Lane," cooed Mother,
tucking me up until I was stuck
between tight expanses of linen. Her hair

brushing my cheek, she kissed
me and left me to sleep's certainty.
Yet I felt bereft, accursed:
the highest spot in my county

was not Dunstable Downs
which other children climbed
at twilight. I trod soft dunes
of disenchantment, loose-limbed

and foolishly, fatally lost
among cold winds, sharp hail.
How I would endlessly lust
after Bedfordshire's wooden hill.

Free Will, Amsterdam

"Have whatever you want: boys, girls, dogs,
no questions asked." I asked a question: "Where?"
He would provide the address – some smart
suburban house. "You pay at the door and stay the night."
I enquired if you got breakfast. "Ja," he grinned,
"full English breakfast." I crossed the street
to lean on a canal-side railing. The city did not appear
close to moral bankruptcy; it looked livelier
than I felt. Two corpulent Americans
(he with an expensive camera, she with a crocodile
shoulder-bag) began talking to the pimp. That second
the animals might be consuming dishes of offal, the children
reading storybooks while awaiting their first punter.

Close by stood a medieval church.
Inside, a wooden Christ hung his head and raised
his arms to where sculpted nails were hammered
through each palm. His eyes were bleary
with pain and grief. He croaked drily. I neared
to catch his dying words. "Have
whatever you want," he moaned. I waited to hear
of the retribution attendant upon my mischoice,
but the grained lips were still, as was the rib cage.
I walked out into the entrepreneurial evening,
confused as never before. The tout
was still loitering, mouth loose and moist,
eyes fixing me with questioning intensity.

Listening to the Tapes

Dylan, reading, was a fraud –
sounded like an English priest,
sounded like a loaf of bread
    made with too much yeast.

I'm quite happy with his face
– proletarian, up to scratch,
average product of his race –
    but his tones don't match.

Sounded like a High Court judge,
sounded like a half-chewed sweet
left, until it will not budge,
    on a chapel seat.

Fire and brimstone. 'Oxbridge' vowels.
Leaving out his Swansea lilt
made him sound like raging owls
    full of primal guilt.

I'd have liked the boyo more
if roots showed in what he said,
not just any ocean's roar
    going through the head.

Darkness, doom, and drink combined
to bring Dylan to his knees.
Shame he sounded so refined
    in such lines as these.

If each windy, preachy note
had not held such solemn sway
in his sadly striving throat
    he'd have been okay.

Royal Visit: Midlothian Council House

Dalkeith, Friday. A modest crowd.
Press photographers and Special Branch.
Here comes Charles Philip Arthur George
unlike yesterday when he graced tabloids
in a baseball cap. He is slightly stooped
as if from humility. Onlookers clap.
The venue has been vetted assiduously
(Was the resident's grandfather a Marxist?
Have any of his children been arrested?
Does his woodshed grow marijuana?)
and the Defender of Faith is sanctified
by a sun which shines like a new penny
with mum's head on. The all-in-one
Duke of Rothesay, Earl of Carrick
and Baron Renfrew, Lord of the Isles
and Prince and Great Steward of Scotland
pushes open the gate and wanders down
the crazy paving past an honour guard
of petunias. "Come in," says the resident
so quietly he could have laryngitis.
His guest obliges, looks around as though
entering Aladdin's Cave, and mutters
"Wonderful" with apparent sincerity.
The Lord Lieutenant, a Captain of
the Royal Victorian Order, follows stiffly,
ornamental sword scabbarded.
The room resembles a florist's.
On the table a plate of digestives waits.
The curtseying housewife straightens
and trips off to brew some Glengettie.

Anglo-Welsh

This is where you belong:
somewhere in between.
The places you will visit
are those to which you've been
but that's all right because you do
not want a change of scene.

Full-blooded patriotism
remains contention's bone.
You'd rather not hoist any flag
except that of your own
writing. You like dawn and dusk,
the border's twilight zone.

Is it a mirror or
a two-way piece of glass?
Could Alice walk through it the way
that light rays deftly pass,
or does identity fade out,
cloud-shadows over grass?

We're nearly someone else.
Living on the edge
is an uncertain business,
the thin end of the wedge,
a promise not quite honoured,
a shakily held pledge.

But this is where you'll stay,
this anteroom, this half-
way house. You hear old ghosts
incredulously laugh
because the lines of history
are falling off the graph.

Fly in a Hospital

The bluebottle, in helmet and goggles, circuits the ward,
a mad aviator who will end up in Casualty. Beds glide past
like battleships rising out of the mist of a warm sea;
on board, the infirm drift towards the horizon of their pain
or the sure footfall of land. It stops. Plaster of Paris
is warily explored by six legs; oiled suckers
scale the smooth incline that coats a tibia, until
a launch towards the menu of new discovery:
four-star restaurant of the sluice, chic diner of damp sheets.
Everywhere nurses frown like distracted doormen
at its presence; its appetite is frequently denied
by waving hand, brandished magazine. Rumour has it
the basement contains a delicatessen of cold meat,
name-tags gracing big toes. For now, shrivelled grape
and crumpled tissue suffice, though it hopes
for a used dressing before the day is out. Wings
beat on, conveying it to the curtailment of desire:
gorged satisfaction; exhaustion locking it to a ceiling;
houseman's irritated swat. Until then, to cruise
is to live, chained to the freedom of hunger and disease,
magnetised by bound wound and drained groin,
sickened by its own aerial insistence.

Reprieve

You're there already in a sense:
the swirling tunnel with a light
attracting you. It has been since
the world began. You can't be late
though can be early. Then a face
will tell you it is not your time;
you must return to all the fuss
of living. So the fusty tomb

or shining urn again awaits.
"He's coming round!" a staff nurse shouts.
"We thought we'd lost you." Stiff and white,
you stare up from the crumpled sheets,
wishing yourself beyond this realm
of boredom and inconsequence,
back where the mind can safely roam,
and feeling bitter as a quince.

"You should be grateful," someone crows
a few days later. Home again,
you watch some movie with Tom Cruise
zapping the enemy, and groan.
Death is much better than this state
of imperfection, compromise,
and longing. You unwrap a sweet
and stare into the actor's eyes.

Swimming the Atlantic

My parents were of this world,
chained to it. The words thronging their heads
throng mine. They took for granted the nonsense
of Christmas cards, and handshakes,
and combing their hair before meetings:
gestures, among countless others, by which
proprieties were maintained. They knew hope
– or thought they did. Neither was equal
to the immensity of death. They were small
and friendly, like the average day;
they consumed; they could have been accounted
on the side of the angels. What possessed them
to stand on the shingle at dawn, old, grey,
shivering, and – protecting only their decency –
cast off into black water? It was too big
a frame for their tiny canvases; they were
tunes on a penny whistle, not symphonies.
Yet enter death they did: up to the neck,
grimly and purposefully pursuing a crawl
which, compasses said, would lead to America.
I waved them goodbye. They were reluctant
to depart but seemingly had no choice.
Eventually their heads were ambiguous
as waves corrugating the Channel's surface.
My wife and I gathered up their belongings
and walked back to the car. We were both
silently weeping. Salt tears.

Last Throes

Below Monmouth the Wye is dying,
writhing piteously on its bed of pain.
From lofty Plynlimon it raced, young
and lively; it was to attain
a settled middle age among
the fields of Herefordshire, flowing

sturdily onwards; but now it is lost
among dark hills, brooding as if
knowing it approaches the estuary
which will deprive it of life
and purpose and identity.
Some sour threshold has been crossed

and it turns this way and that between
the great walls of its confinement.
This is beautiful, some say,
but tragic too, and silent.
Who is there to understand its agony,
its letting-go when lost to the Severn?

Others affirm this is the grace of maturity,
the gentle curving of old age,
turning its cheek to the sun, then turning
the other cheek; but only rage
trapped by circumstance greets the discerning
onlooker, awesome in its purity.

Incorporeal

My life as a ghost is neither here nor there,
a lift stuck between floors, where physical
phases into indescribable. No book remains
a cumbersome research tool. I am
in among its pages the moment I see it, siphoning off
its strength like a kid with a milk shake.
I drink libraries. Too often there is insufficient time
to savour the experience, because I am on the highway
in the back of a '56 Buick, two strangers chatting
in front. I know every recess
of their mind, past and future, summed up
in the tear droplet I can never quite express.
Then it is dawn, and the dew
is doing it for me: Fran Schwartz's
clapboard house along Oberlin Road (Raleigh,
North Carolina, down from the YWCA).
That Sunday when I was invited for tea
and to meet guarded, bemused parents:
here are the chink of those cups, the kuchen,
the Saratoga trunk in her bedroom to transport
personal effects to the gothic wonderland
of Duke University. But she is gone
as if someone had pulled the plug
in a washbasin; try as I might, the maelstrom
will not contain us both. This is
the testimony of a man who hurries to catch
the train of the moment and will not be still.

Beetle

Flat-four air-cooled overhead-valve.
Affectionately nicknamed Lucy.
These colour photographs solve
the riddle of her disappearance
years ago: a scarlet lady
with a bent aerial and numerous dents.

Finally we parked her on the lawn
at our last semi, unobtrusively behind
the breeze-block garage, someone
with a heart of gold and an odometer
reading which could astound,
whom nettles would eventually cover.

Rust? Yes. Sagging seats.
A smell of the boot cupboard. Nonetheless
her chrome smile lasted, a weathered glitz,
and her big round eyes gazed innocently out.
December 1980: we found a smart address.
The neighbours would not have welcomed her to it.

She glints forever in my mind
as if she were as good as new.
Here we are – Metz, or maybe Dortmund –
heading south one warm July
during our lost youth, me and you
and a doughty motor that cannot die.

Settling Mother

I park the wheelchair and activate the brake. We have
an unspoken routine, punctuated by sighs. She clasps
as if shipwrecked against the Old Rugged Cross,
and settles with the hint of a smile, light returning
to troubled eyes. Where is that cradle, kept beside
the bed, from which she lifted a mewling bundle
to clasp against her breast in a representation of
eternal motherhood? Her breasts are desiccated now;
her sexuality is a dried riverbed. We are victims
of an uncommitted crime. No one hates us, yet we feel
dispossessed, robbed of our youth, herded into the ghetto
of age, condemned to deportation. One day I shall stand
beside this mattress, and on it will lie an effigy,
a wax Madonna. Then I will straighten, look again,
and see only the whiteness of new linen, a shroud
laundered for its next occupant. What is obscene
is not this context for grief but its inevitability.
All the cleverness I can devise is unpicked
by fingers which do not exist. The worst enemy
is the insubstantial one, the fear, the threat,
the shadow's shadow. What I dread is not the hourglass
and its unstoppable silent tumult, but the last grain.

Suspended Animation

I watch the hours come round
and wonder what you're doing.
The still air makes no sound.
There could be trouble brewing.
I'd never know. Were there
the chance of distant viewing
I'd take it, and I'd stare
with psychic force, perceiving
your mood, your state, your hair
and clothes. I'd be receiving
some evidence about you:
your entering, your leaving.
But I must live without you
now... perhaps forever.
I love and never doubt you
and wish we were together.
I know we share the minute.
I know we share the weather,
the day – and all that's in it –
and yet we are apart.
The flügelhorn and spinet
are closer in their art
than we in our mute music.
The beating of your heart
stays close. I cannot lose it
in my imagination.
I feel your pulse. I choose it
to soothe my consternation:
unrelieved, profound.
Another day is dawning,
another senseless morning.
I watch the hours come round.

The Annual Convention of Russian Undertakers

I could not fault the hotel. After the flight all we wanted
was to relax. My bride of six hours held my arm
with nervous anticipation, though I too was as edgy
as any Westerner, unused to the Cyrillic alphabet
and the unsettling trappings of grandeur, despite
concrete's attempts to discredit past opulence.
The view from the National gave us Red Square
to admire and St. Basil's floodlit cathedral.
Its large restaurant yielded formal waiters,
barmen with brilliantined hair and a razor parting,
plus a hundred brooding guests, few with their wives.
Soon they might loosen ties, glaze eyes
with vodka, and exchange hearty backslaps;
now all that could be heard was the fateful chinking
of soup spoons and the slurping of bullfrogs
from the Siberian marshes. That night, as we lay
in a well-appointed room in each other's arms,
facing the future with British buoyancy
and the unquenchable optimism of young love,
six sombre shapes materialised around the bed
as if at the funeral of an apparatchik, hands
loosely linked in front of them, saying nothing
because there was absolutely nothing to say.

Between Baroque and a Hard Place

Where innocence meets mischief, *putti* reign,
their mindset
not quite passion or gain
but an indistinct state
of legerdemain.

Prick-teasers, go-betweens, the type of
younger brother who galls
through chirpy insistence, these love
envoys have compact balls
and penises and won't shave

for years. They get beneath your feet.
In their eagerness to please
they irk. Eye-catching, indiscreet,
they resemble show-off pageboys
after weddings: at

once adorable and execrable,
the sort of little shits
who crawl under the table
to undo shoelaces. It's
only because they inhabit fable

that we tolerate their excesses
and even envy their
chases, embraces,
and romps *en plein air*
wherever caresses

are the currency and sweet nothings
the speech of the chatty.
Beyond their forgettable mouthings
they shower confetti
and petals and proffer gold rings.
Cheeky amoretti!

Belsen Funeral Urn

Branches stir in autumnal breezes which dispassionately
scud over Lüneburg Heath, yet the sound is wrong:
choir of cheese graters, cacophony of death rattles.
Nightingales, say the old, inhabited these woods.
They were at home here as nothing has been since.
Their lieder were bittersweet, a distillation of hopes
and memories whose flow was stanched by jackboots,
the juddering-to-a-halt of cattle trucks.
Evenings are easy at the villages of Winsen and Wolthausen
but enchanting melodies are no more. An elderly woman
empties an ash can in the corner of her yard. The wind
blows history into her face. She closes her eyes to it
and stumps back indoors. Where are the Ashkenazim,
their lullabies as bright as birdsong? Where is
the chutzpah of children playing on cobblestones,
the schmaltz of vintage tunes on a violin?
I sit in my neutral Saab, shut out the world,
slot in a CD. Respighi: *The Pines of Rome*.
At last a nightingale pierces the air,
though at the Villa Borghese.
Dusk silhouettes sepulchral trees.
Their boughs are hands
trying to draw down music from the skies.

Talking to the Wallpaper

I've been doing it for thirty years,
asking the floral patterning for protection,
petitioning the great god Anaglypta
– usually in private. Its powers
are universal, stronger than the sun;
its unwritten laws (*lex non scripta*)

control everything. Kneeling, I face
the horizon of the dado, wondering
what lies beyond: new worlds, or just
hard paste? Many refuse to fuss
with the stuff, straightforwardly preferring
paint. Sometimes I fancy I can see Christ

among the curlicues, the tendril forest
of my belief, at other times the Tempter.
When guests stay they see nothing
other than reproduction William Morris.
They say it's better than distemper
though call my prayer-life hollow mouthing.

Let them. Jesus had his flock:
I have mine... feel its texture
with the flat of your hand. Alone,
I go to church; the feedback
there is entirely different. I address a mixture
of oak and brass, lead and stone.

Dangerous Enchantment

We started thinking about each other too often.
Although attached to our respective spouses, we required
the *frisson* of adventure, to recapture that flirtatious spirit
once taken for granted. When I began dreaming about her
I knew she was growing under my skin, a tumour
which promises new life. I wondered where I might be free
of my obsession but she was everywhere.
At any hour she would arrive, flushed and breathless.
Petulant wild child. Release. Torment. Yet she accused me
of being all these things and more. I awoke:
she lay beside me. I focused: it was my sleeping wife.
I shaved: she was in the mirror. I breakfasted:
her photograph was in the newspaper. She was
every woman on the way to work. I had to see her again,
just as I knew she would have to see me.
I went round to her house while her husband was away.
Hollyhocks. Crazy paving. My heart in my mouth.
She answered the door, surprised, more beautiful
than ever, and asked me in. Alone in the kitchen
we said nothing, sensing there would always be
too much to say and too little time in which to say it.

Rex

Our dog went off to find a place to die
beyond the hollyhocks, beyond the dahlias,
down into the dell – where it could lie

and think of nothing. I will count my failures
and small successes when the hour is near;
but he expired where masses of azaleas

fill the mind with colour, banish fear,
and show the spirit heavenliness already.
The song thrush was a lusty balladeer,

the breeze was balmy, spring was holding steady.
I dug a shallow grave and placed him in it;
removed his collar. Although stiffly dead, he

was still my friend and would till my last minute
warm me with his understanding eyes.
He'd sensed my heart and knew that he could win it

even in puppyhood. Each day's surprise
welcomed an energy that remained boundless
until the final month. Now the house sighs

and settles in its sorrow; hope is groundless
currently. Here hangs his useless leash;
there stands his basket. My distress is soundless
and absolute. No mirage. No pastiche.

Greenland Literati

You cannot bin your invitation to the annual party.
Lars will be there with his woman Mimi,
both squiffy on arrival. Niels will greet you
with malodorous breath. Karen's cleavage
will command attention. They'll have written nothing
as usual. Initial high-mindedness will dwindle
to gossip after the chilled akvavit
with its follow-up of Tuborg and marinaded herring.
Henrik will slap your back with fake camaraderie:
"How's the modern saga progressing – or shouldn't I ask?"
Riposte with a query about his planned haiku.
Poul will again lament Godthåb renaming itself Nuuk.
Poor old Carsten will go on about his blockbuster
which has the gestation period of a mammoth.
And, yes, a pecking order is discernible.
The cards of personality rarely get shuffled.
We know who agrees with whom that Mogens
should remain spokesperson, were anyone to listen
beyond their coterie, their chairs and glasses.
Meanwhile, the ice sheet crumbles into the ocean.
Plants grow with increasing variety.
Consider transferring your dubious devotion
to the up-and-coming Agricultural Society.

Punch and Judy

It doesn't have to be like this.
We could be friends. It could work out.
We could give enmity a miss

and atomise our awful doubt.
But who blinks first? Whose pride allows
the other to raise victory's shout?

Neither. We resort to blows.
The children cower in their rooms,
raised hands shuttering their eyes

to no avail. When evening comes
we sulk, mired in our ditch of hate,
trapped in the debris of our dreams.

Wedding photographs relate
how it was before the storm,
the blackened eye and fractured plate,

the comically wielded broom.
A policeman and an alligator
add complexity, yet seem

superfluous. Each holidaymaker
laughs at our discomfort, then
drifts away. We meet up later

in a wicker hamper, when
darkness cloaks our raggedness,
our jangled nerves, our ceaseless pain,

and trade more insults. Where's the end
to what the world consumes with glee:
our fractiousness? Oh let's be friends,
you bitch! For Christ's sake, let's agree.

Regression Therapy

It was like the city of Darwin: warm, humid,
down under. It was like scuba diving, which we did
in the Gulf of Carpentaria – outboard motor a heartbeat
eighty metres away, the pilot and his mate
on shark patrol. It was wonderful, isolated
and insulated, trapped within the freedom
of liquid light and calming depth, and you would gladly
never have resurfaced had not hunger,
oxygen depletion, and the conditioning of walking,
talking, and earning imposed their pull.
You heard, permeating this beauty like a stingray,
a countdown, after which you would come round,
no longer in prenatal suspense, and the hypnotist
would say you had been there again, the state
before birth, and you would scan the dry walls
of the cool office and crave maternal cosseting,
that Gulf, that womb, that long ago. Reluctantly an adult,
you would agree to another session in three weeks' time,
another chance to unravel the string of the psyche,
the knotted airline which had threatened to stop
your rising trace of bubbles, your buoyant tomorrows,
bursting through surfaces....

The Bearded Lady and the Manikin

I have to clip it every other week
so that unruliness is obviated.
Many would call the sorriest of freaks
a whiskered woman, yet I do not hate it.

I'll give you a Vandyke with waxed moustache,
a goatee, or a classical display
like Freud or Chekhov. Primitive or posh,
I'll be a caveman or a popinjay.

The circus is my life. I travel round
with groomed eccentrics, never stopping long.
My lover is a dwarf. Whilst not profound,
he's witty and reliable and strong.

Secreted in our lustrous caravan
we complement each other perfectly.
He is no misbegotten Caliban
but someone warm and generous. When we

lie together in the hirsute darkness
we have no equal. The abnormal earth
turns beneath us in its ancient starkness
while we share an accommodating worth

you would not understand. I clasp his tiny,
wondrous body and he strokes the hair
which elevates my features with its shiny
curliness. We are the ideal pair.

I am the father whom he never knew;
the mother also. He's the son I crave
though cannot form. We rise above taboo,
me with my perfume, he his aftershave.

The Guy from West 72nd St.

I'm going to the John Lennon concert
at the International Arena. He last
played Cardiff in the mid-eighties.
The ticket includes a night at the Hilton
on Kingsway. When I was twenty
my grandfather, an old army sweat,
couldn't abide him ("Scouse idiot;
needs an 'aircut"). Now my grandson
recoils ("Geriatric rocker. No, thanks").
He spans my life, a psychotropic rainbow.
The cat's-eyes down the road we share
shine like no other; it's almost
a psychic bond, somewhere between
chatoyant and clairvoyant. We'll hear
predictable songs from the sixties
right up through his nineties' albums:
Heavenly Lite, Do You Still Knead
The Dough – a dig at McCartney,
home baker and galactic superstar,
Apple Laws (run the words together
for an ovation). The backing group
will be professional and slick.
The audience will submit from the first note.
He'll exude confidence, though the fire
has dimmed since that incident outside
The Dakota – where he still lives –
when a thirty-eight iced his wife.

41

The Anniversaries

(Whitebrook, Monmouthshire)

All are dead, the old ladies
who used to beam reassuringly
at our unease. They had always
been that age, like the sea,
enthusiasm in waves
up the chapel aisle. Christ saves

boys from drowning in tweeness,
I'd hoped. Little white collar,
polished black shoes, a heinous
Brylcreem shine: you stood there
reciting pious doggerel
which usually went down well.

An awesomely perfect girl
– flouncy ribbons and bows,
a lacy unreal whirl
of confection, retroussé nose,
clean knickers – would stand up next.
We were angelic unsexed

dwarves. A royal court
would have loved us. Some Spanish king
would have given us sweetmeats, bought
tutors, and everything
would have been lutes and oysters
and darkling Moorish cloisters.

But this was fifties' Wales
in a valley few had heard of.
The walls were mosses, snails,
and rising damp. No word of
progress might filter through
ever. Nothing seemed new.

Life was tinged with the eerie.
We were askance and wary....
All that has gone for ever,
yet no beauty, pain, or rage,
nothing grown-up or clever,
can rival that makeshift stage.

Against Stereotype

Two fitters install a kitchen in our suburban home:
twentysomething, muscular, earringed, jaunty...
yet their ghettoblaster plays Grieg. I note a scattering
of other CDs - Albinoni, Fauré, Orff - and double take
at their vocabulary: Craig uses 'juxtaposition',
Jason 'totemic'. Only then do their movements register:
rarefied, balletic, though not mincing or effeminate.
Craig holds his screwdriver with the sensitivity
of a portraitist; Jason plies his mallet with the precision
of a Christie's auctioneer. I sigh as Peer Gynt
fills the room, and crane to discover whether it is,
as suspected, Karajan who wields the baton.
My admiration peaks when they break for lunch:
no white bread sandwiches, crisps, chocolate bars,
but salade niçoise, Gruyère, iced coffee soufflés.
They knock off punctiliously at five, exiting
with a Restoration flourish. The room is depleted
by their passing, the house palpably colder.
The cul-de-sac withers as their van leaves it.

Money Spinner

"Of course you can do it, and no one will know
who threw the coin to the sidewalk below.
A thousand apartments are ranged round the square;
a dime zinging wildly through Manhattan air
could come from wherever. And if it connects,
well, it's better than booze and the next thing to sex."
He took a projectile out of his jeans.
He was handsome and beefy, a rich kid from Queens,
and wholly amoral. "The assholes down there
are ant-like, expendable, nothing to care
about in the slightest." He spun the hard disc,
irrespective of where it might carry its risk
of serious injury. It disappeared
as soon as he'd thrown it. The moment was weird.
We were feisty and young and the morning was bright
but packed into his action was darkness not light,
an infinite darkness, a split-second thrill
which could lead the same week to a mortician's bill.
 "Ah, no motherfucker has bought it today,"
he said disappointedly, then turned away
from the veranda and went back inside
the up-market living room. Boredom not pride
had rewarded his effort. He hadn't caused sorrow.
"No matter. I'll send down another tomorrow."

Unresolved

At last he would say where the family treasure
was buried. Although he had sworn to carry the secret
to the grave, now that his time had come
he tugged me closer. "Jot this down," he rasped.
"The village where I met Mary in 1958.
Take the Llanfihangel-Bryn-Pabuan road.
It's under common land. Go on a Sunday in May
early: there'll be no frosts to restrict your spade.
Lash rope around the chest once it's found
and tie the other end to your towbar...."
The curtains shot back. A hard-faced sister explained
that drapes should stay open. She consulted her watch
and beckoned. "Doctor's rounds are next.
You must leave immediately." I straightened, anxious
about losing the thread which led through generations.
"Not yet," I said, but she manoeuvred me by an elbow
towards the exit. I ended up in a corridor
holding the scrap of paper, wondering if
I had spelt Llanfihangel-Bryn-Pabuan correctly
and who Mary had been.

The Wasp Trap

Rather than swat the critters, risking
tennis elbow or smashed crockery,
I'd go into the kitchen, asking
mother for a jam jar that was empty

yet sticky still, then punch a jagged hole
in the lid. Soon the container would
sit on our doorstep or a windowsill,
half-filled with water. I would watch like God

while insect after insect buzzed my way,
attracted by the ghost of a preserve,
settle, and crawl (the best part of the day)
into the aperture. Their treasure-trove

would prove to be illusory; they would
seek an exit, all to no avail.
Next morning before breakfast I would stride
up to their confinement, for a whole

mortuary of corpses to reward
my avid gaze. The safety this would bring
was worth the ugliness. With gratitude
I'd sneer at them 'Hey, death, where is your sting?'

I stopped the practice when my father broke
the silence of three decades to declare
that his old man, a patriotic bloke
from Middlesbrough, a tough submariner,

had died when a torpedo'd hit the hull.
All his colleagues in that iron lung
had drowned off Pentland Firth. Thereafter, full
of doubt, I almost welcomed being stung.

In the Club

Dave is pregnant. He has been inseminated by lager.
We guessed it might happen. Those trips to the British Legion
finally paid off; regular unprotected drinking
reaps its reward. Yet he seems proud of his profile
beneath the Benidorm paternity shirt. During these special days
he can dream of the years ahead, how his habit
might turn out, whether he will be the grandfather
of double chins. Women get it over with quickly.
For Dave such expectancy is like a Christmas puppy:
a gift for life. I pat him on the shoulder, careful not to ask
when the big event might be. Mothers-in-waiting knit
bootees and provide a layette; Dave plays darts unconcernedly.
The room's fug will, he feels, not distress the unborn;
nor will his nightly pie-and-chips lie too heavily
on his diaphragm. Is he preparing a name for it,
or will he wait to discover what it is before committing himself?
I don't ask him that either.

A Rude Awakening

I used to hear my parents making love
just as, years before, they had made me;
I used to hear each gasp and creak and thud,

the ghostly soundtrack of that mystery
adults indulged in. I could only guess
at what they did. They'd finally break free

and sink through silence as I sank through blackness,
terribly alone, alert, and tense.
I did not share their covert smiles and slackness,

their realm of wonder and their common sense.
Terror was mine in that exploding darkness;
it ringed my mattress like a barbed-wire fence.

At breakfast the next day all trace of starkness
had disappeared. Flowers decked the table.
Father read the paper. Mother's dress

was crisp and fresh. And somehow I was able
to be the son they wanted me to be.
Their passion was a dream, a monstrous fable,

dispelled by toast and cereal and tea.
The clock ticked on the mantel. The dog yawned.
We were as calm as the Sargasso Sea.

Another morning had uniquely dawned.
England was at peace. Two butterflies
giddily cavorted on the lawn,

drunk with exuberance. My father's eyes
remained expressionless. A few crumbs lay
on mother's lap, between her secret thighs.

One Careful Woman Driver

It's a happy car.
I rarely drive in fourth,
to save the engine.
I call it Charles,
quietly, in case other cars
or owners get jealous
and break our special bond.
Primitives believed the world
is sentient, that stones
and trees are equally
animate. Think of those
wonderful elements which
inhere in my car.
They are similar (if
in different proportions)
to my own. I confess
to mollycoddling Charles.
I overpolish. It may
be a common failing.
He's drunk on oil
and wax. His bright-
work can hurt the eye
with its gleam.
We all know unfortunates
left to their own devices:
the insolvency of rust,
the trickery of pinking.
Charles gets serviced
with expensive regularity.
Even the garage admits
I am far too lenient.
One mechanic said, "Give
him some stick. Seventy
along the motorway would
iron out his wrinkles."
I stood, surprised.
Charles has no wrinkles.
I have seen to that.

A Change from Southsea

A holiday in Hell! We'd won the prize.
The competition spiel had caught my eye:
A Fortnight In A Place Where No One Dies.
Those Of A Nervous Cast Need Not Apply.

The Nether Regions was a fine hotel.
The food was always steaming. My sole frown:
I had to tell the kingpin – Jezebel –
I could not turn my radiator down.

The room had a four-poster bed, and beams,
and was as long and high as it was wide;
double glazing neutralised the screams
that wafted from the racks and wheels outside.

As theme parks go, the place was pretty samey:
different types of torture without cease.
Even the demons yawned, though the more gamey
kept things fresh through insight and caprice.

The them-and-us perspective did not yield.
Pity was not felt in these environs.
Ingrained evil acted as a shield
although the victims writhed and wailed like sirens.

Only when we left did great compassion
shake me by the shoulders. Until then
my gait was spry, my features were not ashen,
I felt no sorrow for my fellow men.

The days passed quickly. Every photograph
showed hopelessness, excessive pain, or fear.
I sent my neighbours postcards for a laugh:
A spot beyond compare. Wish you were here.

Shell-Shocked

*(An egg has been stolen from a swan's nest
in Pittville Park and replaced with a lager can.)*

Cheltenham protests.

A watch is belatedly mounted.

Battle-hardened veterans stare into their gin.

Gaiseric, king of the Vandals, has led his hordes
down the A46 from northern lands under cover of darkness;
from the council estates' Ultima Thule
Wayne and a few mates have made the incursion.

Barbarian shadows fall across the Pump Room's
Ionic columns. A cold breeze buffets the Rotunda
along Montpellier Walk. Holst's great planets
murmur in the firmament.

"Betcha 'aven't got the bottle to!" Lee taunted,
tattoos eerie in the moonlight.
Wayne belched, and dived into the lake.
A Warhol replaced a Brancusi.

Ripples have spread across the town in recent days.

Clatter of armour and hoof, flap of pennon,
hysterical neigh of steed....

The iconoclasts move on.

Dead of Night

(Three months after his fiancée's burial
Roberto Carlos da Silva, 21, of Sorocaba,
Brazil dug up her wedding-dress-clad body
and consummated their relationship. He told
the Estado news agency: "I was desperate
and needed her.")

Glint of moonlight on a spade.
Cicadas active in the grass.
Slow progress yet a hint of speed
in fraught limbs. Beneath that – grace,
a deathless poise, a love that won't
forever be denied. He sees
again her face, fuelling his want

incessantly. Her full mouth says
'Come to me now'. He heeds the call.
She never died but only changed
apartment for sepulchral cell,
renouncing air for earth, the charged
purlieus of the living soil.
She still can laugh and cry and bleed,

circling on time's carousel
to claim him as the delving blade
hits hardwood with a nameplate on.
He rests, throat dry, eyes strangely moist.
Reacquaintance will dawn soon:
a woman rising in a mist
of taffeta and chiffon. Then

her beating heart, her breathing lungs,
her breathless kiss. The membrane's thin
between two worlds. She whom he longs
for lies within his grasp, almost,
youth and beauty gently laid
on a silk base. Sweet scent of must.
Strong fingers grapple with the lid.

Remembering Gilda with Bitter Affection

During our relationship I was worried
by your sense of being in other places.
I borrowed you from them. You belonged
to strangers, which made me feel a stranger.
You were warm and endearing and we never
argued, yet when friends drove down from London
you became the self I felt uneasy with.
An annoying rural burr appeared
at the edge of my words, while your voice
was suddenly cut glass and tinkling ice cubes.
Although I was introduced as your partner,
throughout those excruciating weekends
you had eyes only for sophisticates who swilled
Corbières in our kitchen and scoffed cassoulet,
relishing the goose I had killed with difficulty
and prepared with tears. Then you were gone,
without a gram of acrimony, leaving
an explanation I could hardly fault
but not, like your first letters, subtly scented.

The Mauve Tam-o'-shanter

It wasn't meant to start like that:
my sister's best friend in a hat
plucked from her head on Elie beach
        by strong Fife breeze
and me – in reckless hot pursuit –
its rescuer. The deed bore fruit
beyond all expectations, each
        signed up to please

the other for a lifetime. Lurch
of bells in an Anstruther church,
reception at a festal hall,
        a honeymoon
in Norway: these grew from my act
of chivalry. Last year, attacked
by something terrible though small,
        you hummed our tune

exhaustedly – then closed your eyes
on three decades, our nuptial prize.
Oncologists could do no more
        than shake their heads;
and so a journey once begun
so flippantly reduced to one
man gazing at a polished floor,
        the fateful bed's

occupant as still as stone.
I held your hand. The ancient bone
beneath the flesh had been there since
        the dawn of time:
you were an immemorial fact
which none could cancel. Our staunch pact
could not be broken. None could rinse
        away the rhyme

and reason of that Elie beach
with everything within our reach:
the home, the kids, the rich years spent,
        our maiden kiss,
and a blown hat I deftly caught.
Those numbers don't add up to nought.
And yet I sense it wasn't meant
        to end like this.

A Pony Struck by Lightning

It was galloping right to left, north-west
to south-east, over a wet field in Wales
with only two houses visible in any direction;
and the muffled thunder of its hooves receded
then advanced as the curve it described
brought it to its end. A flash on its forehead.
Light in its eyes, then darkness. The haunch
rippling as the life ebbed out of it. The heart
suddenly a stone simulacrum. No film
exists of this except the one I run inside
my head; usually it plays itself, a black-
and-white movie in a small arts cinema
with one customer in the stalls. The mane
flowed, and the angle of bank was almost
the trajectory of the circus horse bounding
around the big top, a swimsuited girl standing
on its back. Her white teeth. Her blonde hair.
Her feeling that nothing could displace her.

Welterweight

The burnt-out bruiser tracks you with his eyes.
His red, bucolic face inscrutably
occupies the same place every night.
He wants you to speak first. Once cornered, he
will rarely be outboxed. He just sits tight
and reminisces. There is no surprise

about the way he speaks; excitement's gone.
His big fists, soft as babies', hardly stir.
The game's betrayed him; yet, above the bar,
he – tigerish – glares down from yesteryear,
unconquerable, deathless as a star.
Mostly to himself, he mumbles on

about his victims, how the crowd would stand
and cheer him to the echo, how he met
Tommy Steele, Farouk, and Cyril Lord,
how all the letters of the alphabet
combined to sing his praises here, abroad,
in every real, imaginary land.

His glass is seldom empty. Single malts
fill the evening, mixed with Malvern water.
His misty eyes are vulnerable, sad.
"I 'it 'im 'ard. I never give 'im quarter."
You nod and murmur, "You were quite a lad."
How long can he sustain these new assaults,

these alcoholic onslaughts? "He's all right,"
the barman mutters. "Never any trouble.
He didn't marry, and he lives alone
with loads of ruddy ghosts." I find a table
across the bar, and sit down on my own.
His eyes trace my uncomplimentary flight.

Dark Horses

Eight of us are pony-trekking in mid-Wales,
sloughing suburbia for the rigours
of Mynydd Eppynt. A group identity
develops. We lodge off the beaten track.
The weather is uncertain, the sky dramatic.
She is a barrister's wife. Kent diverts her
with domestic scenarios; London provides
theatres and restaurants; this allows her
to dress down: old cords, baggy jumper,
hair held by a scarlet ribbon. He is Laurentian,
of indeterminate history, sullen as clouds
before rain. Their compatibility is,
on reflection, entirely natural:
she the unbuttoned sophisticate,
he the brooding stranger.
On night three her bed is visited.
In the next room I hear abandonment.
My blankets permit little warmth.
The beasts are restless in their stalls.
The mountains lour like strange gods.

Chauvinist Verse

The trouble with poetry now
is that too many women are writing it.
From San Francisco to Slough
their streetwise jottings extend.
Perhaps we men are inviting it.
Back when I was a lad
it was Wystan and Louis and others.
Though some of the stuff was bad,
on most of it you could depend.
It wasn't done by their *mothers*.

The Robert Conquests have gone
into the shadows, as have
the Charles Madges, the John
Lehmanns, the Henry Treeces.
Under the spotlights weave
other celebrities, skirted,
lipsticked. From Harvard to Hitchin
innumerable assorted
sisters, aunts, and nieces
have flung down their wares in the kitchen

and taken up baring their soul.
The feminist and the toughie
strut their stuff. On the whole
it's okay, I suppose, but Rex Warner
rather than Carol Ann Duffy
is what I am used to. Girls
used to be so compliant.
The Susans, Shirleys, and Avrils
who knew their place in the corner
nowadays are defiant.

It makes one feel uneasy.
There appears to be little hope
that things will improve. These queasy
feelings may have no end,
thanks to Adcock and Rumens and Cope
and the rest of the uppish bunch.
The virus is out of the lab.
It's already come to the crunch.
Most chaps on whom one could depend
are somewhere under a slab.

Belle-Île

One Monday morning in Morden, waiting for
the Northern Line to absorb him, he craved
an island off Brittany like a pregnant woman
needing chalk or raspberries.
                              The platform
shrank to the head of a pin.
                              He stood among
its dancing angels and reckoned he could get there
by sundown: Heathrow – Paris – La Baule
then the relinquishing of the hired Mégane
at Quiberon ferry terminal.
                              An aversion to
Underground trains and fluorescent offices
was entering his bloodstream.
                              Later that day
an alter ego arrived at a *pension*,
shady in worn Burberry and Bogart fedora,
closing down the past like a computer.

The Sadist's Children

We were the sadist's children. Every year
we settled down before the Christmas tree
on the special morning, drained of cheer
because we knew precisely what would be
inside the gift-wrapped boxes. Still he made
us open them. Mother sat, tight-lipped,
afraid to speak or stay his hand, afraid
of every footnote to life's manuscript.

Father, eyes as bright as any rat's,
followed our doomed movements with a glee
that almost overflowed. No cheap ersatz
present met our gaze. No gewgaw. He
filled each box with nothing yet again.
Our countenances did not fall. We knew
well in advance how to short-circuit pain
by staying deadpan. Once, out of the blue,

each wrapping yielded an expensive toy.
Recoiling, as in horror, we let slip
our brotherly sang-froid. Was this a ploy
or a new start in our relationship?
Wonderingly and slowly, out we lifted
the great surprise: a train for each of us.
We turned in gratitude, uniquely gifted,
and thanked him for his unexpected kindness.

We played for hours with unrestrained delight
and by that evening, having dropped our guard,
were different children; but that very night
he took our trains and smashed them in the yard.
We woke up the next day and raced downstairs.
Mother would not face us. Father grinned,
our eagerness the answer to his prayers.
Outside the pieces rolled round in the wind.

Simone

The afternoon is falling to pieces
like a lifted jigsaw. Morning
fell into place like a kaleidoscope.
Noon saw the turning, your hand
through a carriage window, waving....
Along Boulevard St. Germain there is
a space beside me, you-shaped.
Pedestrians stroll by, as through
a ghost. Already your face is
flashing past far fields, a white bird winging
towards another home.
Paris is full of women. Many
share your birthday, your forename.
All have features vaguely similar.
What, then, do I miss, if not
a part of me you carry within you:
a human locket holding a breathing photograph.

Augury

Assembled celebrities make small talk while they wait
within the hotel ballroom. Showing my face at eight,
I'm instantly in charge. "Take a seat," I say.
Beyond us Surrey twilight rounds off a perfect day.
"Do not ask for details. Be mindful of my words.
Death is on the wing like a flock of butcherbirds.
James Dean, when they give you those Porsche ignition keys
chuck them in the gutter and take a taxi, please.
Isadora Duncan, send every scarf you own
to some deserving person or let it out on loan.
Lawrence of Arabia, forgo your motorbike.
Lock it in the coal shed. Be cool and businesslike.
Do not let bad judgement draw you to its use.
And, dear Charlotte Brontë, avoid coition's noose
or you will die while pregnant, according to the tarot.
William Rufus, with your visor, guard against an arrow.
Keep away from methane if your surname's Plath.
Oh, and Agamemnon, do not take a bath.
Ted Kennedy will offer a ride (you could go far)
but Mary Jo Kopechne, don't get in that car."
Guests have started mumbling. I hope my help is heeded
as sharp-eyed divination indicates it's needed.
Yet Marie Curie radiates health, and so my warning
is taken with a pinch of salt. "We'll leave here in the morning,
thankful for your message," she says. The others smile.
Perhaps they think I'm crazy. They'll keep my fears on file
then go about their lives with a foolish, carefree air.
I point at each of them in turn and simply say, "Beware".

Exploit

The most exciting thing I ever did
was crawl a mile underground
with Lyndon Morris in 1957
along a flue tunnel from a Victorian
paper mill, long since abandoned,
in a forested valley in Wales.
No one knew we were there.
When we emerged into the twilight
our whoops ricocheted off
surrounding trees. Some nights,
even now, I lie awake and imagine
the rockfall in that Plutonian passage,
how nobody heard our screams,
how we were never found.

At the Literary Party

You do not know how brilliant you are.
You buttonhole a hexagrammoid star.
He's tousled, teddy bearish, and dependable;
you talk of Hampstead, heartburn, *Babi Yar* ....
She's human. She's divine. And she's upendable,
the celebrated poetess from Dunstable
or somewhere. Daring. Not afraid of guff.
Her energy is monstrously expendable.

And there is whatshisname who writes that stuff
no one can understand. It's glitzy, rough,
unflaggingly enjoyable, pure crap:
he never knows when he has said enough.
Now chatter to this unassuming chap
who translates from the Basque without mishap.
He holds his Merlot so close to his chest.
Here's a potential ally. Worth a slap.

Before you can evaluate the rest
some woman clears her throat and hollers. Yes,
tonight you'll hear that grand Australian
read his latest sonnet. Well, I'm blessed.
A hush descends (though somebody goes gaily on
they soon dry up). It's about Arthur Waley on
the playing fields of Rugby. Now *there's* topical.
Yes. Very good. We like it. Saturnalian.

It's getting loud in here and somewhat tropical.
People drift away. That's fairly typical
around this stage. The last *bonnes bouches* are bitten.
It almost seems like savagery to stop it all
but real life beckons. Poems must get written.
Ciao. So long. Vehicle-laden Britain
lures you from this sanctuary. You traipse
out into the night, back to Thames Ditton.

Was it worth it? Somebody from Cape
said *Do ring.* It could have been. Your grapes
sooner than you think might yield good wine.
All you need's a publisher. The apes
have yet to realise you're genuine.
And so you go on sending stuff to Tyne
and Wear or Huddersfield or Potters Bar.
You do not know how brilliant you are.